Euripides

IPH...

A new version from the Greek of
Iphigeneia in Aulis
by Colin Teevan

Introduction by Edith Hall

OBERON BOOKS
LONDON

First published in this translation/adaptation in 1999 by Nick Hern Books

Reprinted in 2002 by Oberon Books Ltd.
(incorporating Absolute Classics)
521 Caledonian Road, London N7 9RH
Tel: 020 7607 3637 / Fax: 020 7607 3629
e-mail: oberon.books@btinternet.com

New reprint 2004

A catalogue record for this book is available from the British Library.

ISBN: 1 84002 303 1

Cover image: Andrzej Klimowski

Printed in Great Britain by Antony Rowe Ltd, Chippenham.

1005926717

for Madeline

Contents

Introduction

Edith Hall

Since the late 1960s Greek tragedy has been performed more often than at any time since Greco-Roman antiquity. There are several obvious reasons for this renewed interest in these extraordinarily powerful theatrical classics. Our own moment in history seems to have found in them a particularly truthful mirror in which to examine its own reflection, to contemplate at a slight artistic distance its own painful social and political problems. The questions which we find the ancient Athenian playwrights asking with sometimes astonishing candour involve such modern social dynamite as the power struggle between women and men, the nature of parents' rights over their children, and conflict between different political, ethnic and religious groups.

One of the most conspicuous interests which modern culture shares with the society which produced Greek tragedy, Athens in the fifth century BCE, is an ambivalent yet obsessive fascination with the causes and effects of war. The twentieth century saw greater and more devastating wars than any other period in human history, wars whose lingering aftershocks are still felt the world over. Other military and paramilitary conflicts have for decades failed to find solutions; the world is becoming all too familiar with the phenomenon of teenagers like Iphigeneia, volunteering to seek glory by committing suicide in the name of causes which they have never been trained to think about from anything but a partisan perspective. Euripides' fellow Athenians, likewise, were almost permanently at war; they trained their young men to welcome a patriotic death on the battlefield, and their young women to produce sons to die systematically and unquestioningly in the name of their ancestral constitution. For the entire quarter-century immediately preceding the first production of *Iphigeneia in Aulis* in 405 BCE, the Athenians had been almost continuously at war with Sparta, their deadly enemy in the Greek-speaking world. They had fought dozens of battles and lost thousands of men. They had exterminated whole cities who had dared to revolt against them, committed execrable atrocities, and peremptorily exiled and even executed several of their own generals. They had also suffered the humiliating occupation of much of their own territory by Spartan militiamen, and a short-lived but terrifying coup during which they had lost their democracy altogether.

In *Iphigeneia in Aulis* Euripides responds to his experience of an extended and terrible war by producing perhaps his greatest war play, greatest precisely because the violence it portrays is ultimately left both unjustified and unjustifiable. Euripides leaves absolutely no possibility of plausibly excusing the murder of Iphigeneia by appealing to the notion of a 'just' war against an alien or aggressive power. The atrocity around which the tragedy revolves is the premeditated slaughter of a wholly innocent victim who shares not only her ethnicity and religion, but even the closest of family ties, with her persecutor. In the teeth of the most desperate opposition from his articulate and loyal wife Klytaimnestra, Agamemnon sanctions the ritual killing of his eldest daughter, an inexperienced, unmarried teenage girl who should have been able to rely on him as her protector. Colin Teevan, the author of this striking new version of Euripides' play, is an Irish dramatist living and working in a country long torn by internecine violence. But he is also a husband and father. It is scarcely surprising that he has found in this ancient text an ideal arena for reflecting on the hypocrisy and lethal destructiveness inherent in the posturing and rhetoric of violent public men.

Iphigeneia in Aulis was first produced just a couple of years after Euripides' own death, at the spring festival of Dionysos, in the god's own theatre on the Acropolis of imperial Athens. In the year after its production, 404 BCE, Athens finally lost her war with Sparta, her democracy, and her pride. This most pessimistic of war plays was produced in a group with two other of Euripides' tragedies, including one of his greatest masterpieces, *Bacchai* (a tragedy which Teevan has translated for the National Theatre). It is strange to reflect that the actor who in *Bacchai* originally played the role of the Dionysos, tutelary deity of theatre, will in the course of the very same spring morning also have had to impersonate Agamemnon, king of kings, war criminal, and hypocrite. The chorus who played Dionysos' retinue of bloodthirsty maenads, ecstatic devotees of his cult, will also have had to play the role of another frenzied group of sexually excited young women, Greek adolescents turned on by the specious glamour and paraded masculinity of the Greek heroes gathering at Aulis for their armada against Troy.

Not everyone in this tragedy has been seduced by the idea of the glorious soldier. One of the most shocking moments in Greek tragedy occurs at the point in this play at which Klytaimnestra appeals to her husband and co-parent Agamemnon in a desperate attempt to dissuade him from sacrificing their daughter. She opens her argument with the information that Iphigeneia is not the first child of hers whom Agamemnon has killed. Klytaimnestra says that she married him against her will, after he murdered her first husband, tore her baby from her breast, and dashed him to the ground.

Although the other Greek tragedians, Aeschylus and Sophocles, also dramatised episodes from the same archetypal myth, this horrifying piece of information appears nowhere else. The nasty little secret is a typically Euripidean touch. It turns out that Agamemnon, the brilliant military strategist and respected monarch, has actually always been capable of slaughtering innocents in his own self-interest. Euripides has turned a tragedy about Agamemnon's famous dilemma over Iphigeneia – whether to prioritise public or private interests – and shown what such a so-called 'dilemma' means in terms of real human relationships. His high-sounding moral impasse is reduced to a single sordid incident in the life of a self-serving warlord. At the same time Euripides exculpates almost completely one of the most famous villainesses in the Greek tragic repertoire, Klytaimnestra, by portraying her as the serial and blameless victim of an abusive husband.

Klytaimnestra finds the strength to resist Agamemnon, and implies that if he kills their daughter he may himself be killed on his return from Troy. That is, she threatens him with the plot of Aeschylus' famous *Agamemnon*, a masterpiece which in 405 was half a century old and certainly familiar to Euripides' audience. Teevan has seen the importance of this crucial 'inter-textual' detail within Euripides' treatment of the story. He frames his version of *Iphigeneia in Aulis* with scenes from Aeschylus' *Agamemnon*, which dramatises the revenge Klytaimnestra does indeed take on her husband a decade later. Teevan thus empowers Klytaimnestra, by showing the moral (or immoral) agency of which Agamemnon's abused wife is later capable. Such a dramaturgical device is a modern expedient, but in fact it is wholly in keeping with the psychology of *Iphigeneia in Aulis*, a tragedy in which almost all the characters are strangely conscious of their futures, or at least of the futures of the characters they become in the dramatic tradition. This highly literary feature lends the play an unusually modern – indeed postmodern – tone. The inclusion of the tiny baby Orestes, for example, who will grow up to become the revenge hero *par excellence* in several famous tragedies, forces the audience to 'remember the future' even as the device recalls Agamemnon's tragic family's already tragic past.

Euripides was fascinated by the factors which condition the moral choices made by individuals, and in his tragedies repeatedly explored the dangers inherent in precipitate decisions. Athenian history provides several examples of such decisions taken in time of war; in 427 BCE the Athenian democratic assembly furiously voted to execute all the male inhabitants of the island state of Mytilene, only to revoke this horrible decision at an emergency second meeting called the very next day after 'a sudden change of heart' (Thucydides, *History of the Peloponnesian War* 3.36). This moral uncertainty and emotional volatility resulted in a desperate race against time as one trireme chased another across the Aegean sea. *Iphigeneia in Aulis* uses myth to force its audience into contemplating a similar occasion when decisions with life-or-death consequences were taken, rescinded, and reinstated by unprincipled and cowardly warlords during a military crisis.

Aristotle complained in his influential treatise on tragedy, *Poetics* (54a), about the 'inconsistent' characterisation of Iphigeneia, whose understandable rejection of the plan to kill her is subsequently replaced by a passionate death-wish. It has been suggested, in defence of Euripides, that Iphigeneia's predicament has virtually driven her insane. But she is only imitating the male characters in her own drama. Agamemnon has summoned her to be sacrificed, changes his mind, but changes it back when Iphigeneia's early arrival forces his hand; fear of his own army's reaction is far stronger than love of his daughter. Menelaus changes his mind no less dramatically, emotionally rejecting his early arguments (nauseatingly couched in the language of expediency and pragmatism) when he is infected by his brother's distress. Even Achilles, outraged by the sacrifice scheme, allows a traumatised girl scarcely out of childhood to persuade him that she really wants to die for her father and fatherland. It is not so surprising that this sheltered youngster should collude in the militaristic ideology of the community in which she finds herself, when the strongest warriors in Greece are incapable of moral reflectiveness or even maintaining a consistent position for more than half an hour.

The overall impression made by Euripides' play and by this contemporary version is identical: it is of a community in absolute moral crisis. The prospect of Iphigeneia's death is unbearably moving, but it is inseparable from the tragedy's portrayal of the volatile Greek mob, manipulated by sinister, unseen spin doctors, and above all the self-delusion and cynical duplicity practised by the community's self-styled leaders. Iphigeneia's problem is simple. It is how to die nobly, in an ignoble cause, for the sake of utterly ignoble men.

Ever since those last dark days of the fifth century BCE, the eloquent, painful *Iphigeneia in Aulis* has found admirers and translators. During the Renaissance, when ancient Greek began to be read widely in the West, humanists were fascinated by the close parallel between its portrayal of the child sacrificed to appease wrathful divinity and the Old Testament stories telling of Abraham's attempt to sacrifice Isaac, and of Jephthah's immolation of his beloved only daughter. But even they realised that the Euripidean version drew the most stark, sensitive and uncompromising moral picture. Indeed, *Iphigeneia in Aulis* was the first Greek tragedy ever to find its way into an English vernacular version: an aristocratic female prodigy, Lady Jane Lumley, translated it into her mother tongue as early as 1558, and (appropriately enough) presented the translation to her father. *Iphigeneia in Aulis* also inspired one of the most influential of all neoclassical adaptations, Racine's *Iphigénie en Aulide*, in 1674, and an important lyrical opera of the same name by Christoph Gluck exactly a century later. But over the two centuries since then the sheer horror of the daughter-murder, combined with an increasing reluctance to see young women as no more than their fathers' extensions or chattels, has rather kept this most painful of tragedies away from public stages; in our post-feminist times the task of converting this ancient play into modern theatre requires artistic commitment, courage and an unswerving ability to look atrocity in the face and stage it without sentiment, titillation, or melodrama. Translating the vigorous, pointed, naturalistic poetry of Euripides has always been a challenge; producing a fresh and performable version which does not traduce the original, but still succeeds in making sense in a modern socio-political context, is a considerable achievement.

Durham, May 2002
Professor Edith Hall holds the Leverhulme Chair of Greek
Cultural History at the University of Durham, and is
Co-Director of the Archive of Performances of Greek and
Roman Drama at the University of Oxford

Characters

OLD MAN

AGAMEMNON

MENELAUS

KLYTAIMNESTRA

IPHIGENEIA

ACHILLEUS

CHORUS
of young women from Chalkis

This version of *Iph...* was first performed at the Lyric Theatre, Belfast on 2 March 1999, with the following cast:

OLD MAN, Donncha Crowley

AGAMEMNON, Sean Hannaway

IPHIGENEIA, Morna Regan

CHORUS LEADER, Niki Doherty

MENELAUS, Richard Dormer

KLYTAIMNESTRA, Paula McFetridge

ACHILLEUS, Kevin James Kelly

Director, David Grant

Set and Costume Designer, Gary McCann

Lighting Designer, Paul O'Neill

Movement, Richard Knight

Music, Debra Salem

The play was subsequently produced on BBC Radio 3.

*Night. The roof of the citadel at Mycenae, the evening of
AGAMEMNON's return from Troy.*

Old Man

You Gods,
Cut me loose from this life of tears!
A man should pass his dying years in quiet rest,
Not banished to the roof to keep the watch;
Ten whole years, bag-eyed and sleepless,
I've lived here like a dog, distancepeering.
For what? For fire. For the victory flames
That were to tell us Troy is trashed and taken
Now they have come,
Beenandgone this morning dawnlight.
But though it's come,
Though we have won,
Though peace is danced
Through ruined ghetto streets
And Agamemnon now sleeps safesound in his bed,
I cannot shut my eyes.
I have forgotten how.
War breeds inhuman habits in the most humane of man,
And my habit was to storytell nightlong to the stars –
My faithful friends.
I've longlost care for man;
A crazy, wild, warlusty beast.
So, I tell the stars the scraps of tales
Longforgot now by the world.
Though muddled, half-remembered in my wrinkled head,
They sometimes make good hearing.

(*A chuckle that turns into a yawn.*)

The stars, they like to laugh
At the hero deeds of men.

(*Pause.*)

No, they do not give a damn for us,
And peace has come, or so it's cried,
And there's no longer need to watch.

17

(A crash of celebration.)

You Gods,
Must I dig one more nightmare
From the ashes of the world?
Must, it seems, if ever am to rest.
Where does it begin, then, this last tale of mine?
In day long gone, in Aulis
Where the sons of Danaos,
The daring Danaan Greeks,
Had gathered to set sail for Asiatic Troy.

Agamemnon
(Off.)

Old man! She comes for me.

Old Man

Yes, I was an old man, even then,
And Agamemnon called for me
As he is calling now –

Agamemnon
(Off.)

She comes with a butcher's knife
Old man! Wake up.

Old Man

Ten long years ago.

> *(Ten years previously. The Greek camp at Aulis.*
> *AGAMEMNON stands in front of his quarters.)*

Agamemnon

Come quick, please, old man!

Voice

This is such joy, Papa,
It's so long since I've seen you.

Agamemnon

Iphigeneia...!

Voice

It was so sweet of you to send for me.
Father, put off that troubled face

And let me see your loving eyes.
Forget your cares
And be with me awhile.

Agamemnon

Iphigeneia let me rest.

Voice

Forget your cares –

Agamemnon

O Gods, I've not the strength –

Old man! Wake yourself
And come quick to my quarters.

Still the sea and still the sky
And silent the winds, still, at Aulis.
Dawns white light has not yet cracked dark night;
There is still time to turn –
Leda, Tyndaro's wife, bore two daughters;
My Klytaimnestra, and Helen...
That same Helen, whom every ghettoman of Greece
Desired to make his wife.
So sharp and keen our jealousy,
Violence, dread death and enmity,
Each man swore upon the other.
Murderous we grew toward each other.
Till Tyndaros, her father, wondered how,
Without provoking civil strife,
He might marry off his daughter.
Thus he decided:
Make every Danaan suitor to a man,
With solemn binding covenant, swear
To stand by whosoever won her hand
Should any man – Barbarian or Greek –
Try to lure her from her husband's bed,
And to raze that bastard's village, town or ghetto
To the earth. This we agreed.
So did Tyndaros entwine
Each man's fortune to the next,

Then bid his daughter to decide
Which Danaan warman she might have.
My brother, Menelaus –
That they had never met!

But, for a while, all seemed to hold together.
Life went on. Our oaths slipped from mind. Until,
Until, that is, there sailed from Barbarian Troy
Paris, Priam's son,
Who with his fancy foreign dress
And honeywords, seduced Helen,
Then stole her, the fairest spoil of Greece, home,
Home to savage Troy.
Well, Menelaus, a man possessed,
Tore through all of Greece
To remind us of our solemn covenants,
Insisting we redress the wrong.
And so the Greeks have gathered at this bay
– Aulis – armed with spear and stick and swords of shining steel
And strong prowed ships as swift and fell as sharks,
And, because I am my brother's brother, I suppose,
They have elected me to lead this lunge on Troy.
If truth be told I'd now forego this fameglory.
Old man come here!

(OLD MAN has arrived.)

Old Man

Forego fameglory?
Is to be Grandmaster
Not the dream of every Danaan,
Agamemnon Anax?

Agamemnon

So you have woken from your dreams, I see.

Old Man

I do not dream.
Sleeplack stings my eyes like acid.
It is my years that make me slow.

Agamemnon

I am jealous of you,
I'm jealous of all honest Johns
Who journey through this life
Unrecognised, unrenowned and ...

Old Man

Unrewarded?

Agamemnon

Unknown.

Old Man

These words are hardly worthy of a warman.
You were born a son of Atreus,
Born to bear the burden of high office.

Agamemnon

Well now I would forego it.
This windless weather stays our boats
At anchor here in Aulis.
The gathered Greeks grow mutinous.
They itch for action. They'll brook no more delays.
While Kalchas, the lord high holyman,
Interpreting our stalled momentum, has determined
That for us to sail to Troy
Iphigeneia, my girl, my child, my own daughter,
I must sacrifice to the stonehearted huntress,
Artemis.
When I first heard this, I resolved
Without delay, to disband the Danaan force.
But Menelaus with fierce yet wily words
Persuaded me the only course
Was to proceed with this dread deed.
And so I wrote to Klytaimnestra
To send me our daughter and her dowry,
Saying she was to marry Achilleus
The sea-goddess Thetis' son.

Old Man

And would Achilleus, cheated of a bride,
Not wreak a fierce revenge?

Agamemnon

Fierce and dread, he would.

Old Man

Then you're dead, too?

Agamemnon

He knows none of this; few do.
Kalchas, for now at least, keeps it to himself,
While Achilleus lends his name
But not his knowledge.

Old Man

Still and all, a dread design;
You promise your child she'll marry Achilleus,
While you really plan to kill her –

Agamemnon

No.
That is why I've written once again,
And that is why you must leave now with this letter.
I have changed my mind.
Menelaus, Helen, the troops and Troy itself
Can all be damned.
This letter countermands the last
And tells Klytaimnestra keep
Our daughter safesound at Mycenae.
You were bonded as a servant
To my wife and therefore me,
You alone I trust of this inconstant crew,
You alone are friend to my family,
So forget your years and fly.

Old Man

I'll speed, as best my bones allow.

Agamemnon

Do better.
Drive yourself past limitation,
And go directly there.

Old Man

I am your dutiful domestic.

(*Exit OLD MAN.*)

Agamemnon

Dawns white light cracks night's black.
Hurry, I said, while there's still the time for turning back.

(*Exit AGAMEMNON. Enter CHORUS of young women
of Chalkis.*)

Chorus

Our fathers restrain us,
They try to train us
To be their dutiful daughters,
But we skipped our homes
Beside the foams
Of Arethusa's virgin waters.
We hiked our way
Around the bay,
From Chalkis on the strait,
To catch a sight
Of the Danaan might
Which will Troy annihilate.

Troy they will sack
And bring Helen back
From Paris that Barbarian.
Revenge is the food
To put our heroes in the mood
And Greece will overcome.

As we neared our quest
We stopped for a rest

In the grove of Artemis' shrine.
A stone was stained red
With the blood of the dead –
The huntress's heavy fine.
A flicker of shame
In our hearts did inflame
At our dark desires;
To see the great warmen,
The noble Danaans
And their ships,
    And their swords,
        And their spears,
            And their skills,
                And their skin,
                    And their strength,
                        And their, and their, and their –

            (*Crescendo.*)

Troy they will sack
And bring Helen back,
From Paris that Barbarian.
Revenge is the food
To put our heroes in the mood.
And Greece will overcome.

Chorus Member

Look!

Chorus Member

Where?

Chorus Member

Over there –

Chorus Member

Ajax!

Chorus Member

Ajax who?

Chorus Member

Does it matter?

Chorus Member

Yes. There's two.

Chorus Member

Ajax son of Telamon and –

Chorus Member

Ajax son of Oileous.

Chorus Member

One a deadly freedom fighter –

Chorus Member

And one a dirty womaniser.

Chorus Member

Which one's he, then?

(*Wolf whistle.*)

Chorus Member

Can't you tell?

Chorus

Deadly!

Chorus Member

Well who's that there, then?

Chorus Member

Where?

Chorus Member

Discussing his discus-ing.

Chorus Member

Diomedes, of course.

Chorus Member

Def –

Chorus Member

Tres def –

Chorus Member

He's dynamite –

Chorus

A bang!

Chorus Member

I guess.

Chorus
(*To CHORUS MEMBER.*)

Huh?

(*Pause.*)

Chorus Member

And that's Meriones.

Chorus Member

Son of Ares.

Chorus Member

God of war?

Chorus Member

God, the bod!

Chorus Member

He'd do for me. He's deadly.

Chorus Member

And there's Odysseus!

Chorus Member

Odysseus?

Chorus Member

He's odious –

Chorus Member

Dirtbag!

Chorus Member

Slimeball!

Chorus Member

Scum!

Chorus Member

No he's not!

Chorus Member

Yes he is!

Chorus Member

No he's not!

Chorus

Yes he is!

Chorus Member

Well I'm telling you he's not!!!

Chorus Member

Look! I don't believe it!

Chorus Member

It's him!

Chorus Member

My love. My heart's desire.

Chorus Member

It's a dream –

Chorus Member

A dream come true!

Chorus Member

I'm going to faint –

Chorus

It's…it's…it's ACHILLEUS!

Chorus Member

Achilleus!

Chorus Member

Son of Thetis.

Chorus Member

Achilleus!

Chorus Member

Son of Peleus.

Chorus Member

Demi-God Achilleus!

Chorus Member

Semi-clad Achilleus.

Chorus Member

What a dreamboat!

(*CHORUS look at her.*)

Chorus Member

Fleet-foot Achilleus!

Chorus Member

Freedom fighting Achilleus –

Chorus Member

Formidable –

Chorus Member

Fabuloso –

Chorus

IT'S FUCKING ACHILLEUS!

Along the shore he races,
Like a god he clear outpaces
Beast and mortal alike.
He alone could destroy
Those Barbarians of Troy
And that blow for our freedom strike.

Our fathers restrain us,
They try to train us
To be their dutiful daughters.
But we skipped our homes,
Beside the foam
Of Arethusa's virgin waters.

Troy they will sack
And bring Helen back,
From Paris that Barbarian.
Revenge is the food
To put our heroes in the mood.
And Greece will overcome.

(*Enter MENELAUS dragging OLD MAN by the scruff.*)

Old Man

Menelaus, Menelaus, give it back –

Menelaus

Draw back you wrinkled dog, or you're deadmeat.
You're too loyal to your spineless master.

Old Man

That is to my favour, not my fault.

Menelaus

If you dare carry through such damnblast duties,
I'll favour you with such a fist
You'll soon see the error of your wilful ways.

Old Man

It was not right of you to read the letter.

Menelaus

It was not right for you to bear
Such words of treachery as these.

Old Man

Argue that with Agamemnon,
But let me deliver the letter.

Menelaus

I'll not give it back.

Old Man

And I'll not give it up.

Menelaus

I'll give your baldhead such a beating,
You'll give it up or die.

Old Man

I am prepared to die; it is my duty.

Menelaus

A wholesome homily, for a dog.

(*MENELAUS beats OLD MAN.*)

Old Man

Agamemnon, Agamemnon Anax.

(Enter AGAMEMNON.)

Agamemnon

You gods! What is it now?

Old Man

I am wronged;
By force he takes your letter from me.
Your brother does not love you, Agamemnon.
He goes against you and your family –

Menelaus

My words are more weighty than this old fool's.

Agamemnon

Then tell me, Menelaus,
What eats you now?

Menelaus

Look me fullface and you will know.

Agamemnon

Would I, our father's son,
Fear to face you, Menelaus?

Menelaus

Then why the letter?
What of these words written here?

Agamemnon

What words? I must read it if I am to know.
Give it to me, Menelaus.

Menelaus

Give it to you, Agamemnon?
Not before I show all the Greeks
The duplicity you dare.

Agamemnon

Where did you seize him?

Menelaus

I was waiting, watching, on the road to Mycenae.

Agamemnon

Why did you feel the need
To mind my business, brother?

Menelaus

I sensed that I would need to,
And I am not your servant, Agamemnon.

Agamemnon

This world is in some state,
When a man's not master of his home.

Menelaus

You are a sideways schemer, Agamemnon,
You've always been.

Agamemnon

I'm warning you, I am Grandmaster still,
Head of all the warmen. That includes you.

Menelaus

Then let me hold a mirror to that head of yours,
And don't you in lofty disdain turn from what is true.
I, for my part, giveword to be fair.
You recall how hard you canvassed
To command the warmachine to Troy?
You needed no more fameglory
But lust for power knows no satisfaction.
So, you grasped at every rabble hand,
You kissed their mewling kids with tireless affection,
Your door was open wide to every slave's demand.
You promised one and all the earth,
And, fair enough, you got the job.
But then, Agamemnon, you aboutfaced.
No more did you seek out your supporters.
In fact, you hid behind locked doors,
Sulking like some child here in your quarters.
Office should not alter any man,
You should stand by your friends,
You are where you are now because we put you there.

When I saw how you had changed, brother,
I saw you weren't the man I'd marked you for.

So it's no wonder then,
That when the Greeks came here to Aulis,
Your command began to crumble.
The Gods stilled the western winds;
The warmen, restless, itching for a fight,
Began to voice their discontent.
Some demanded you disband the fleet.
How downjawed you appeared;
What point in all that politicking
If you could not lead our strong prowed ships on Troy?
You asked me, your brother, what to do.

Agamemnon

With a clever word or two
You'll make your own duplicity seem right.
But you've had your say, now it's my turn.
You being my brother,
I'll be evenhanded in my words;
A Grandmaster must maintain
His coldblood and calmbearing,
Even when he stands accused.

Tell me, Menelaus, why you storm at me so strong?
Why the savage face?
Who has wronged you, really?
What is it you want, really?
Is it not a wife you want?
A faithful wife who'll do you right?
The one you had, you could not control
And, I'm afraid, it's not for me
To find for you a fresh one.
I'm not to blame for your present situation.
Is your desire to get her back,
So all-consuming, her who did you such a wrong,
That you would reject all that is right?
Or is it simply that you envy my position?
Whatever motive it might be,

It's bound to be a selfish one.
Am I mad if I decide,
After bitter deliberation,
To withdraw my first decision?
Or is it you who is the madman who,
Being rid of her who was your ruin,
Now wants her back again?
Those former suitors of your wife,
Swore to Tyndaros' oath
Out of hope for Helen's love,
Not love of you, Menelaus.
The Gods view such misguided vows as void.
Surely. They must do.
I, for my part, will not throatcut my child.
It is not right. It will not be
That you would once more have your harlot wife,
While my own life be lived out in loss
Through lawless slaughter of the daughter I begot.
I've had my say.
You rage on long as you like.
But in my family's affairs, I'm telling you,
I will be just.

Chorus

Aphrodite comes in the form of a fly
That bites in the night while we sleep.
Some she lets live in a love that is calm,
Some she sucks with passion deep.

Keep our beds, Aphrodite,
When we're wed, Aphrodite,
Free from the gadfly's bite.
Let our husbands' arms
Keep us free from harm
And grant us your good night.

Aphrodite bit the Spartan Queen,
Helen, with a prickling hunger.
For a savage love, she left her home,
Now we are rent asunder.

Keep our beds, Aphrodite,
When we're wed, Aphrodite,
Free from all temptation.
Let a happy home
Be our goal alone.
Save us from damnation.

Chorus Member
That Helen is a traitorous jilt.

Chorus Member
Look what she's brought to pass.

Chorus Member
She must have known what she was doing –

Chorus Member
She just didn't give a toss.

Chorus Member
But –

Chorus
Yes?

Chorus Member
She acted out of love –

Chorus Member
A love so great it drove her
To leave her country and her home;
I feel sorry for her.

Chorus
What?

Chorus Member
I mean... I mean to say...
Her eloping and all the shame
Was caused by Paris's seduction;
And so, I mean, is Paris not to blame?

Chorus Member
She's been talking to the men.

Chorus Member

I've not!

Chorus Member

She's been listening to their tales.

Chorus Member

I've not! I've not!

Chorus Member

She thinks a man could be the reason
A girl goes off the rails.

Chorus Member

I've not! I don't!

Chorus Member

Don't you see –

Chorus Member

Paris, like all men, could not help himself –

Chorus Member

When it came to himself helping himself.

Chorus Member

Aphrodite brought him to her bed.

Chorus Member

He was simply – you know –

Chorus Member

Penis –

Chorus Member

Led!

Chorus Member

Shame –

Chorus Member

Shame on you –

Chorus Member

Don't you know that men –

Chorus Member

They're all the same, men –

Chorus Member

Only one thing on their minds –

Chorus Member

Turning any inch they might be given –

Chorus Member

Into miles and miles –

Chorus Member

Stop it! Stop –

Chorus Member

But we women –

Chorus Member

We should know better.

Chorus Member

Aphrodite points the way –

Chorus Member

Keep your home and keep your man –

Chorus Member

Or be prepared to pay.

Chorus

That Helen is a traitorous jilt,
Now look what she's brought to pass.
She's turned us all against ourselves,
She –

(Pause. Pointing.)

Chorus Member

It's her.

Chorus Member

Iphigeneia –

Chorus Member

And her mother –

Chorus Member

Klytaimnestra Anassa.

(*CHORUS proceed to welcome the women.*)

Chorus

The nature of man differs one to the next,
But right and wrong are always clear.
Let Aphrodite's mystery point us the way,
So we may live forever free from fear.

Menelaus

Iphigeneia and your wife Klytaímnestra.
They have arrived –

Agamemnon

I see, as does every manjack in the camp.
Look how they rush out from their tents
To see what's going on –

Menelaus

They'll wonder why they've come.

Agamemnon

And what am I supposed to tell them?
It's too late for turning back. Too late.

Menelaus

A marriage. A marriage would appear
The likely reason for their coming.
But to whom? They will want answers.

Agamemnon

You Gods,
How cleartell this heartache?
How begin to break the binds
Of these threads in which I'm now entwined?
Some God plays with me and my plans,
His cunning far outwits my petty wiles.
The rabble live with lighter load,
Unencumbered, they can cry
When the fates fuck them around.
Not so us people of position,

We must appearances preserve.
We are the slaves of our supporters.
Trapped helpless in their gaze.
What can I do?
I am ashamed to show my grief,
Yet it is shameful not to shed a tear,
Such misfortunes now enmesh me.
You Gods, were things not bad enough
Without Klytaimnestra coming too?
With what words will I greet my wife?
With what face can I look at her?
A mother must tend to her daughter, I suppose,
On her daughter's wedding day.
Though this father grieves at how
He must give his child away.
My child,
My ill-starred child,
Who will now honeymoon with Hades.
On her knees she'll beg me;
Father, do not marry me to martyrdom, Papa –

Menelaus

Brother let me hold your hand.

Agamemnon

Take it. You have won.
I have lost, lost everything.

Menelaus

By Pelops and his son, our father, Atreus,
I swear I will speak straight to you,
Not to serve a purpose, not from the head,
But from the heart. Hearing you just now,
Two tears tripped from my eyes,
Sympathy and sorrow.
This war of words cannot continue.
I did not wish to wrong you;
I regret it and am with you now:
And this I say to you:
You cannot throatcut your own child
So my concerns succeed.

Why should you mourn so I may smile?
Why should your daughter darkly die
So my wife may look upon the light?
Why break my brother's heart
To win back her who's broken mine?
I'll find myself a new wife, if at all.
I was stupid and selfthinking till I saw,
What it is to kill one's child.
Disband the Danaans,
Wipe your wet eyes;
It is I who should now let tears fall.

Agamemnon

Menelaus, your mercygiving is not missed.
But we have journeyed past the point,
Where once we might have turned.
Fate now forces me to sacrifice my child.

Menelaus

Who now forces such a fate on you? Not me –

Agamemnon

Them. The warmen, the ghettomen of Greece.

Menelaus

Just send her hushhush back home
To the safety of Mycenae.

Agamemnon

However hushed the sending back,
Her arrival here's well known.
And the reason for her being here
Will not be 'hushed' much longer.

Menelaus

I will keep the Danaans calm;
They will never know.

Agamemnon

Kalchas, our holyman,
Owes me no favours nor bears me no love.
He'll broadcast it to the mob.

Menelaus

We'll throatcut him before he speaks.

Agamemnon

But we told Odysseus of our plans.

Menelaus

You command the warmachine, not he;
You must silence all contention.

Agamemnon

But he's a populist,
A panderer to the lowest denominator;
He'll pose as the soldiers' champion,
Playing on their superstitions,
He'll appeal to their basest bloody instincts –

Menelaus

His ambition drives him hard.

Agamemnon

He will standfast with the ghettomen
And say I swore a sacrifice to Artemis
And now I doubleback.
With such appeals he'll lead the lynchmob
To crush the clan of Atreus.
If we fastfoot it to Mycenae, they would follow
And sack the Cyclopean stronghold
And flatten home and family.

> (*Enter CHORUS leading KLYTAIMNESTRA and
> IPHIGENEIA.*)

Chorus

Keep my bed, Aphrodite,
When I'm wed, Aphrodite,
Free from the gadfly's bite.
Let our husbands arms
Keep us free from harms
And grant us your good night.

Agamemnon

Klytaimnestra, wife.
And Iphigeneia.

Iphigeneia

Papa, my Papa.
I beg you not be angry, mother,
That I've run to my father first.
I just could not wait to kiss him.

Klytaimnestra

It is fitting, Iphigeneia,
My first-born always had more fatherlove
Than any of my others.

Iphigeneia

This is such joy, Papa,
It's so long since I've seen you.

Agamemnon

Those are your father's feelings too.

Iphigeneia

It was so sweet of you to send for me.

Agamemnon

I'm not so sure I would say sweet.

Iphigeneia

Father, you don't look pleased,
Though you tell me that you are.

Agamemnon

The man who must command has many cares.

Iphigeneia

I'm here, Papa, forget your cares
And be with me awhile.

Agamemnon

My thoughts are with you all times, child.

Iphigeneia

Then put off that troubled face
And let me see your loving eyes.

Agamemnon

Does my face not show my love for you?

41

Iphigeneia

Yes, but tears tumble from your eyes –

Agamemnon

Our future parting will be long.

Iphigeneia

Why? What is this Troy?

Agamemnon

The place where Paris lives.
That he had never looked on light of day!

Iphigeneia

Then you are going far away and leaving me?

Agamemnon

O Gods. I have not the strength
To suffer this in silence.

Iphigeneia

But you'll soon come home to mother and to me?

Agamemnon

That is what I wish for.
But no longer have free choice to wish.

Iphigeneia

I wish Menelaus and his stupid problems,
I wish all wars and serious things,
Would simply go away.

Agamemnon

Problems do not go away.
They pass from one person to the next
Till they devour those nearest you.

Iphigeneia

Papa?

Agamemnon

Nothing, child.

Iphigeneia

You've been stuck here too long in stinking Aulis.

Agamemnon

And something still prevents our setting sail.

Iphigeneia

I wish you'd bring me.

Agamemnon

You too must make a journey.

Iphigeneia

I do? Where? Will I go with mother? Or alone?

Agamemnon

Alone, alone without any company.

Iphigeneia

You're sending me to some strange place?

Agamemnon

Enough, Iphigeneia, enough.
It is not needful that you know
Our plans for you as yet.

Iphigeneia

Just hurry back from Troy to me,
When you've beaten those Barbarians.

Agamemnon

First we must make sacrifice.

Iphigeneia

And I will lead the dance
Around the sacred altar?
Can I, Papa, please?

Agamemnon

I envy you your child's heart. Now go inside,
It's not right you're seen out here,
Just let me kiss your white hand.
Too soon we will be parted for too long.

(IPHIGENEIA goes in.)

Klytaimnestra

Agamemnon Anax.

Agamemnon
Klytaimnestra Anassa.

Klytaimnestra
I hear Achilleus is some catch.

Agamemnon
What?

Klytaimnestra
I hear Achilleus is some catch,
But I want more facts about his family.

Agamemnon
He's of Asopus's clan.

Klytaimnestra
Asopus?

Agamemnon
What?

Klytaimnestra
He's of Asopus's clan? Come on!

Agamemnon
Asopus who begat Aigina began the line.

Klytaimnestra
And was it man or god or beast,
Who then begat with her?

Agamemnon
Is this really necessary?

Klytaimnestra
A mother must know details
Of her daughter's husbands line.
I'm waiting.
Mortal or immortal?

Agamemnon
Zeus.

Klytaimnestra
No less.

Agamemnon
Aigina begat Aiakos by Zeus.

Klytaimnestra
Good.
What son of Aiakos then succeeded?

Agamemnon
Peleus.

Klytaimnestra
And then?

Agamemnon
Then Peleus married Thetis, the sea nymph, daughter of Nereus.

Klytaimnestra
Curious. And Poseidon permitted this?

Agamemnon
Zeus approved it.

Klytaimnestra
Zeus again, no less.

Agamemnon
No less!

Klytaimnestra
And what kind of marriage had they?

Agamemnon
A marriage most magnificent,
Conducted by the Centaur Cheiron
In the forests of Mount Pelion.

Klytaimnestra
Who was it then coached Achilleus?

Agamemnon
Cheiron. So he might learn
The ways of the immortals.
Such a man is your child to marry.

Klytaimnestra
No less.

Agamemnon
No more!

Klytaimnestra
What ghetto does he keep?

Agamemnon
You gods! He has a patch in Phthia.

Klytaimnestra
Phthia?

Agamemnon
Phthia.

Klytaimnestra
And to this 'Phthian patch' he'll send our child?

Agamemnon
I think he might.

Klytaimnestra
'Might'? Do you have no care for your child's future?

Agamemnon
I can think of nothing else.

Klytaimnestra
When do they wed?

Agamemnon
When the good luck moon is full.

Klytaimnestra
So, you have sacrificed to Artemis,
For your daughter's happy future?

Agamemnon
I am about to. It is the very duty that delays us.

Klytaimnestra
We must do our gods their rites, Agamemnon,
So they do right by us.

Agamemnon
I will discharge all needful rites, Klytaimnestra Anassa –

Klytaimnestra
You – ?

Agamemnon
All marriage rites, that is.

Klytaimnestra
You'll make me unwelcome at my own daughter's wedding?

Agamemnon
When the eyes of all the ghettomen
Are fixed upon us, yes.

Klytaimnestra
Why make the marriage in this way?

Agamemnon
Return to Mycenae. Look to your other children.

Klytaimnestra
Leave Iphigeneia? Who will tend the flame?

Agamemnon
I will take care of wedding torches.

Klytaimnestra
This is not right. You have no care for custom.

Agamemnon
It's not custom for the Grandmaster's wife
To mess down with the men.

Klytaimnestra
It is custom for a mother,
To give away the girl she bore.

Agamemnon
It is neither right nor good that
Electra and your baby Orestes
Be left at home alone.

Klytaimnestra
They are well protected,
Iphigeneia has only me, it seems.

(KLYTAIMNESTRA leaves.)

Voice

Why, Papa? What is this Troy to me?

Agamemnon

I am not an animal.

Voice

I wish Menelaus and his stupid problems,
I wish all wars and serious things,
Would simply go away.

Agamemnon

I have not a heart of stone –

Voice

If I could sing like Orpheus,
Who touched the hearts of stones –

(*To black.*)

Chorus

Soon shall come our men to towered Troy,
To where the Simois meets the sea,
And range their mighty war machine
Across their green and fertile plains.

And there upon the battlements
Her laurel-wreathed head awhirl,
Cassandra wild, dancing possessed
Shall see their fates unfurl;

'Blood shall be spilt, throats shall be slit
The walls shall fall, our temples stripped,
The very stones of Troy shall weep
As women watch their men hacked down.

Just as you waited on the walls
For Paris' return with Helen,
So shall you watch the Greeks arrive
And destroy us with their warmen.

Blood shall be spilt, throats shall be slit
The walls shall fall, our temples stripped
The very stones of Troy shall howl
As women watch their men hacked down.'

May the Gods forbid we ever see
What these women shall and wonder
Which warman's prize must I now be?
All because of Zeus' child Helen.

Blood shall be spilt, throats shall be slit
The walls shall fall, the temples stripped
The very stones of Troy shall howl
As women watch their men hacked down.'

Chorus Member
Look, I don't believe it!

Chorus Member
It is –

Chorus Member
It's him.

Chorus Member
And he's coming this way –

Chorus Member
It's a dream –

Chorus Member
A dream come true –

Chorus Member
I'm going to faint –

Chorus
It's...it's...it's...it's ACHILLEUS!

Chorus Member
Fleet-foot Achilleus!

Chorus Member
Freedom fighting Achilleus –

Chorus Member
Formidable –

Chorus Member
Fabuloso –

Chorus Member

It's fucking ACHILLEUS.

(*Enter ACHILLEUS. CHORUS mob him. Enter KLYTAIMNESTRA.*)

Klytaimnestra

Achilleus, Goddess son, I thought it might be you.

Achilleus

It is I, but who –
Excuse me, but what class of woman are you
That cuts such a finedrawn figure?

Klytaimnestra

I admire your manners, sir, and must admit
That you'd have hardly met my class before.

Achilleus

I have never met a lady
Who would brassneck a Danaan camp.
Who are you?

Klytaimnestra

Klytaimnestra Anassa,
The wife of Agamemnon.

Achilleus

Klytaimnestra Anassa, this is indeed an honour,
But it's not right we're seen like this.

Klytaimnestra

Fastfooting it already? Stay, Achilleus.
Should we not shake hands, at least?

Achilleus

I beg your pardon, but I believe
That it's not right to touch what is not mine.

Klytaimnestra

Of course it's right, since it's to my child
That you are promised, brave Thetis son.

Achilleus

What? I'm lost for words.
You must be mad to –

Klytaimnestra

It is sweet to see the warman blush
To talk of things like this.

Achilleus

Klytaimnestra Anassa, let me assure you,
I have never courted any of your clan,
Nor has ever Agamemnon
Talked of such things to me.

Klytaimnestra

How can this be?

Achilleus

We must find out.
We cannot both be right.

Klytaimnestra

I am the subject of some joke.
Now it is my turn to blush with shame.

Achilleus

Someone plays with both of us, it seems.

Klytaimnestra

Achilleus, I cannot face you anymore,
Feeling false because someone plays false with me.

Achilleus

And to you, Anassa, fare you well.
I'll go ask Agamemnon what he means by this.

(*OLD MAN enters.*)

Old Man

One moment, one moment please,
Achilleus, Aiakos kin, allow me talk to you,
And to you too, Klytaimnestra.

Achilleus

Who is this old man who dares – ?

Old Man

A slave, I'm not ashamed to say,
Fate permits me little pride.

Achilleus

Whose slave?

Old Man

Klytaimnestra Anassa's, herself.

Achilleus

I'll stay a moment more.
So say now what you wished.

Old Man

You two are sure you are alone?

Achilleus

Enough for you to speak. Come on.

Old Man

Might fate and my poor influence
Save her I hope to save.

Achilleus

You won't if you keep wasting words; out with it.

Klytaimnestra

Don't hesitate for fear of me.

Old Man

You know I've long been faithful
To both your family and to you?

Klytaimnestra

You've been a sworn servant many years.

Old Man

And only came to Agamemnon
As part of your due dowry?

Klytaimnestra

You came with me to Mycenae
And have served me ever since, yes.

Old Man

And that I hold your happiness
Above that of your husband?

Klytaimnestra

I know that, so speak, old man.

Old Man

Agamemnon plans to kill your child.

Klytaimnestra

Never! You have grown simple in your baldy-headed years –

Old Man

He intends, with his own sword,
To slit the girl's white throat.

Klytaimnestra

O Gods, is Agamemnon gone completely mad?

Old Man

Sound of mind,
Except in family affairs, it seems.

Klytaimnestra

Does some demon drive him to this?

Old Man

Kalchas, the holyman, determines it
To be the will of Artemis;
The price that must be paid,
So that the Danaans might set sail.

Klytaimnestra

A price that we could ill-afford.
Sick and more sick grows your story.
My poor child, whose own father schemes to kill her – !

Old Man

All so Menelaus might retrieve his wayward wife from Troy.

Klytaimnestra

Must Iphigeneia foot the bill for my sister's sluttery?

Old Man

So it would seem.
The huntress, Artemis, demands her blood,
If Kalchas is to be be believed.

Klytaimnestra

And what intended Agamemnon
By the contrivance of this marriage?

Old Man

So you'd willingly send Iphigeneia here to Aulis.

Klytaimnestra

Child, I've sent you to your death!
I can no longer staunch my tears.

Old Man

Seeing you so cheated of your girl,
Causes me to cry as well.

Klytaimnestra

How did you hear of this horrific plan?

Old Man

I was to take a second letter.

Klytaimnestra

Telling what?

Old Man

Telling you not to send your child.

Klytaimnestra

You gods, what happened it?

Old Man

Menelaus, fearing Agamemnon
Might see the light of reason
Intercepted it, and me.

Klytaimnestra

Do you hear this, Thetis's son?

Achilleus

I hear it, nor do I weigh it lightly.

Klytaimnestra

They misled us with this marriage
While they schemed to slay my child.
What place is there for pride
When my girl's life hangs by a thread?
I beg you on my knees, Achilleus,
You are a mortal, but born of a line of gods:
Defend us, Achilleus,
In the name of her who'd hoped to be your love.
For you I garlanded my girl,
For you I readied her for marriage,
Not knowing I deathdressed her.
Achilleus, your fameglory will be tarnished
Should you not help us in our need.
For though you might not ever marry her,
As her husband you've been named.
No place, no time for pride, Achilleus.
I beg you: save my child from death.

Chorus

With Syrian flutes
And Lybian lutes
The whole of the forest rang,
Through Pelion's groves,
Bacchanalian droves,
To the marriage, danced and sang.

The golden-slippered Muses move
With solemn steps and sing
Sweet songs to Peleus and his bride,
And golden garlands bring.

With Syrian flutes
And Lybian lutes
The whole of the forest rang,

Through Pelion's groves,
Bacchanalian droves,
To the marriage, danced and sang.

And Ganymede beloved of Zeus
Pours toasts to love and life,
While the fifty girls of Nereus
Encircle man and wife.

With Syrian flutes
And Lybian lutes
The whole of the forest rang.
Through Pelion's groves,
Bacchanalian droves,
To the marriage, danced and sang.

As night draws in around the feast
There comes the thundering hooves of beasts;
The Centaurs born half-horse, half-man
Have ridden from their mountain den,
So Cheiron, dearloved by Apollo,
Might foretell what is to follow.

Of a great hero, all are told,
Who will be bright and brave and bold.
This child of Thetis, her little boy,
Will be the greatest Greek at Troy.
Blissful for one day at least
Are all at that wedding feast.

With Syrian flutes
And Lybian lutes
The whole of Aulis will ring.
Through Artemis' groves
In Bacchanalian droves
To the marriage danced and sang.

Chorus Member
Iphigeneia must face self-sacrifice for Greece –

Chorus Member
Unless rescued by the hand of Achilleus –

Chorus Member

Each way a sort of union.

Chorus Member

Each way a kind of fame.

Chorus Member

I'd die to be the battlemaid
Of Greece's handsome hero men

Chorus Member

Just think; as they are lunging into battle
They'd be lunging in for you!

Chorus Member

(*Parodying.*)

Take me, father, Agamemnon,
Slit my white neck for Greece.
Marry me to all my men.

Chorus Member

(*As AGAMEMNON.*)

My child, you know that we are Greek,
And that as a Greek
We must live by our free will?

Chorus Member

(*As IPHIGENEIA.*)

I do.

Chorus Member

(*As AGAMEMNON.*)

And that a battlemaid must,
Like a soldier, choose her fate?
We are not Barbarians
Forcing victims to the knife.

Chorus Member

(*As IPHIGENEIA.*)

Yes, Papa.

Chorus Member
(*As AGAMEMNON.*)
My child, do you choose this quite freely?

Chorus Member
(*As IPHIGENEIA.*)
I do, Papa, yes, yes I do.
So paint your faces with my blood,
My fierce, warlusty men.
And as you risk your necks for Greece,
Remember, mine was slit for you.

Chorus Member
I'd die for Greece –

Chorus Member
Me too –

Chorus Member
I'd die for Greece and more.

Chorus Member
More? What more?

Chorus Member
It's the utter –

Chorus Member
The absolute –

Chorus Member
The ultimate –

Chorus Member
It's so completely very deadly!
(*Pause.*)

Chorus Member
Achilleus will surely save her –

Chorus Member
He is bright and bold and brave.

Chorus Member

She was not raised a calf for slaughter.

Chorus Member

She is Agamemnon's daughter.

(Enter KLYTAIMNESTRA trailing IPHIGENEIA
followed by AGAMEMNON.)

Klytaimnestra

Away, away from me!

Iphigeneia

I beg you not be angry, Mother –

Agamemnon

My child, why do you cry
And look at me with so little love?
Eyes turned towards the earth,
You tumble tears into your dress.

Iphigeneia

Papa, please, put off that troubled face
And let me see your loving eyes.

Klytaimnestra

Look how even still she yields to you,
I must speak for both of us, it seems.

(Pause.)

Agamemnon

What are you two up to now?
What new twist have you planned for me?
It's clear you both conspire –

Klytaimnestra

Agamemnon, answer me straight,
When I ask this one thing of you.

(Pause.)

Agamemnon?

Agamemnon

If your request were reasonable,
Reason you would hear.

Klytaimnestra

Answer me!

Agamemnon

What a God-accursed fate is mine.

Klytaimnestra

And mine, and hers.
One fate awaits us three.

Agamemnon

Whom have I wronged to warrant this?

Klytaimnestra

You have the gall to ask us that?
This is your reasonable response?

Agamemnon

You know. Someone has told you.
Now will we all be blast to nothing.

Klytaimnestra

Well now I know for certain.

Iphigeneia

I wish Menelaus and his stupid problems,
I wish all wars and serious things –

Agamemnon

I can say no more.

Iphigeneia

– would simply go away.

Klytaimnestra

Listen to me, I'll have my say.
I'll speak in simple words,
So you might understand.
The first offence I charge you with
Is that by force from Tantalus,

My former love, you stole me.
You throatcut him and grabbed my child,
Newborn, from my breast.
You then beat that firstborn child to death.
And when my brothers, Pollux and Castor,
Twinborn sons of Zeus, made war on you,
You fastfooted to my father Tyndaros
To plead for his protection.
So you slimed back between my sheets.
I did my duty to your home
And worked, as you must admit,
To make our house a happy one.
Your palace prospered thanks to me.
The hunter rarely bags so skilled a catch.
I bore you three children,
Two daughters and a son.
But, not content, you now intend
To rob me of another child.
And if someone asks you why you killed her,
What will you reply?
So Helen might return to Menelaus?!
It is rich indeed to pay for whores
With your own children's blood.

What will my heart then whisper
When I return home to Mycenae?
When I see my daughter's empty chair?
When I see my daughter's dresses
Hanging lifegone in her room?
When I sit alone and sob,
'O my dead child, throatcut
By him who first did give you life,
Struck down by his and no other's hand.'
What will my heart then whisper?

I swear you will receive repayment
When you return home again to me.
Dare seat yourself at my table
And I will dish you such desserts
As you have never dreamed.

Do not, by the Gods, do not make me do
Such deeds as will damn us all forever.
And what will you beg the Gods for
As you push home the knife?
A fitting welcome home
For such a foul farewell?
For, surely, it will be so;
The Gods, they are no fools,
They do remember child killers.

And what of your other children?
Will you expect to hold them
When you return home from the war?
They would fear to look at you,
Let alone embrace you;
Who knows who would be throatcut next.
Have you thought of this?
Or is political position
Your only real concern?
Why not tell the Greeks,
If they want fair winds for Troy,
Then they should choose by lot
A childkill for great Artemis?
That is right. That is reasonable,
But you offer your own daughter,
While Helen, who's betrayed us all,
Sails safely home to Sparta?
I'm not wrongthinking in these things.
Agamemnon, save your child and family.

Chorus Member

A father cannot kill his daughter –

Chorus Member

She was not raised a calf for slaughter –

Chorus Member

Agamemnon, Agamemnon Anax save her!
If you can, at all, you should.

(*Pause.*)

Iphigeneia

If I could sing like Orpheus,
Who touched the hearts of stones,
I'd sing so every rock and stone
Would beg you not to kill me.
I would sing, but can't.
I have only tears
And these white arms
Which, reaching out to you,
An olive branch, implore you;
Do not kill me.
I am young, too young
And light is sweet to look upon,
In death I would be blind.
I was the first to call you father
And the first you called your child.
I gave you your due fatherlove
And you returned a father's love to me.
Will I one day see you,
You once said,
The wife of some great warman
Happy with your husband and your home?
And I replied, Papa,
That one day I would welcome you
Into my husband's house,
And return to you the labours
Of my bringing up.
I remember all these words
Which you have now forgotten.
For you now want to kill me.
In the name of Pelops
And your father Atreus,
Do not make my mother
Who bore the pain of birth,
Bear this double pain of death.

O, what is this Troy to me?
Who this Paris?
What did I do to him?
Or Helen? How can my death help?

63

Look at me, father, fullface,
So that when I'm dead
You will remember me.

Chorus

That Helen,
Look what she's brought to pass –

Chorus Member

Such young dreams of love –

Chorus Member

Death –

Chorus Member

And fameglory –

Chorus Member

Had we all.

Chorus Member

A father cannot kill his daughter –

Chorus Member

A child's not reared a calf for slaughter –

Chorus Member

In the name of any cause.

Chorus

O, Agamemnon, Agamemnon,
Agamemnon Anax save her,
If you can, at all, do save her
If, if, if –

Agamemnon

Stop!
I am not an animal,
I have not a heart of stone,
I dearly love my children,
I would be mad if I did not.
This thing, this sacrifice I dare to do
Is dread beyond belief,
But not to would be doom absolute;

And so I must.
Look at this vast machine of war,
Look at these bronze clad fighting men;
They cannot budge, we cannot sail
To raze the towers of Troy,
If I don't sacrifice you.
So Kalchas has decreed.
Please understand;
Aphrodite weaves a warlust
Amongst the Danaan men.
Our marriage beds have been defiled,
These bastard Barbarians must be defeated
Once and for all.
Should I ignore the Gods' decree
They'll kill me,
Your mother Klytaimnestra,
Our whole clan.
It's not my brother who enslaves me,
But Greece, whose freedom I must fight for.
Greece must overcome.
Both you and I must give our all
For the freedom of our homeland.

(*To black. IPHIGENEIA and KLYTAIMNESTRA stand
huddled in front of AGAMEMNON's quarters.*)

Iphigeneia
O mother, a crowd of men are coming towards us.

Klytaimnestra
Do not worry,
The frontmost is Achilleus, goddess' son,
The man you were to marry.
He will protect you,
He will save you.

Iphigeneia
Let me leave, let me hide my face.

Klytaimnestra
You tremble, child.

Iphigeneia
I am shamefaced.

Klytaimnestra
But why?

Iphigeneia
Because, such dreams I had –

Klytaimnestra
Grow up, girl, there's not the time.
Our last hope now rests with him.

(*Enter ACHILLEUS.*)

Achilleus
Klytaimnestra, Leda child –

Klytaimnestra
What news have you?

Achilleus
The ghettomen raise a bloodcry.

Klytaimnestra
Why?

Achilleus
Your child.

Klytaimnestra
The bird of omen circles.

Achilleus
They cry for blood of sacrifice.

Klytaimnestra
Did anyone defend us?

Achilleus
I tried to but they roared me down.

Klytaimnestra
They defied you, a goddess' son?
Who would dare?

Achilleus

Every Danaan to a man.

Klytaimnestra

And your own men? The Myrmidons?

Achilleus

Were the loudest.

Klytaimnestra

We have lost all, my child.

Achilleus

They jeered me,
Saying I was lovelost to the girl.

Klytaimnestra

What did you reply?

Achilleus

I said they should not seek
To slay my wife to be.

Klytaimnestra

One man at least remembers
What is right and what is not.

Achilleus

Her father said that she was mine,
When he sent for her from home.
One of us, at least, should honour that.

Klytaimnestra

What did they say to that?

Achilleus

My voice could not be heard above the clamour.

Klytaimnestra

The minds of mobs are animal.

Achilleus

I still intend to save her.

Klytaimnestra

One man against the many?

Achilleus

My servants bring my sword.

Klytaimnestra

You have some honour still.

Achilleus

I only do my duty.

Klytaimnestra

You will stop the sacrifice?

Achilleus

I will try.

Klytaimnestra

And who will come to take her?

Achilleus

The lynchmob, led by Odysseus.

Klytaimnestra

He yields to the people's pressure?

Achilleus

He gladly chose to do this deed.

Klytaimnestra

Some choice to be a childkiller.

Achilleus

I will stop him.

Klytaimnestra

And, when he takes her,
Will he tie her up?

Achilleus

Like a calfling, if he can.

Klytaimnestra

What can I do?

Achilleus

Hold her tight.

Klytaimnestra

Could that save her from the butcher's knife?

Achilleus

Our last line of defence –

Iphigeneia

Mother, Sir,
Please listen to my words.
In vain you try to save me.
It is a fearful thing indeed
To face up to the unfaceable.
But we must.
It is right, Mother, that you praise this man,
But you know we cannot hope to win.
So realise his fameglory
Will be damaged in defending us.

Listen to these words I have to say:
As I've been standing here I've thought,
Thought of that which is being asked of me,
And have decided I must die.
Die for Greece, die for her hero men,
Die famously and freely,
Die by my own consent
With no shallow thoughts of self.
See now how well I speak?

To me all Greece now looks in hope;
To me it lies to launch
Our shining ships on Troy;
To me it now falls to keep
Barbarians from our land.
And by my blood
I'll help to pay back
Paris for his rape.
I must serve Greece,
And so win my own fameglory.

It is not right for one like me
To love this life too much.
Our lives should not be lived
For just ourselves alone.
I was born for Greece not for myself.
Myriad men stand ready armed,
Myriad more sit at their oars;
Greece has been sore wronged
And these Greeks would gladly die
For their beloved homeland.
How can I cry out, 'No,
I do not want to die?'
It is not right.
Nor is it right that Achilleus
Might lose his life for mine;
A warman's life is of more use
For our homeland's cause.
And furthermore, how can mortals
Reject what great Artemis demands?
I have no choice, so choose to die.
Sacrifice me, then smash Troy;
Smash Troy and all those stinking Trojans!
That will be memorial enough.
Women will sing my glory evermore.
It is right we rule Barbarians,
For we are free and they are not.

(*Pause.*)

Achilleus

Though I wish it with my heart,
My head has not the words
To counter you.
But I will set my sword
Beside the sacrificial stone,
Should your will, through fear, weaken
And you cry out for my help,
Seeing the dagger at your throat.

Iphigeneia

Mother, why do your eyes moisten
With a swell of silent tears?

Klytaimnestra

I have good cause;
Heartache now is killing me.

Iphigeneia

You have no cause to cry.
I am saved. I am and will be saved.

Klytaimnestra

How? What do you mean, child?
A mother always mourns
The dying of her child.

Iphigeneia

You need dig no grave for me.

Klytaimnestra

You must have memorial, a resting place.

Iphigeneia

My resting place shall be
The sacred shrine of Artemis.

Klytaimnestra

You have decided.

Iphigeneia

Yes. It is my good fortune
To give my life for Greece.

Klytaimnestra

Do you have any word
For your sister?

Iphigeneia

Tell her good-bye and take care
Of little Orestes.

Klytaimnestra

O, what will my heart whisper
When I return home to Mycenae?

When I see your empty chair?
When I see your dresses
Hanging lifegone in your room?
How might I keep your memory?

Iphigeneia

Do not hate my father,
He still is your husband.

Klytaimnestra

His conscience now will run him
A sore and ragged race.

Iphigeneia

He does not desire my death,
He does it so the Danaans might be free.

Klytaimnestra

He did it by duplicity.

Iphigeneia

It is time.
Young girls of Chalkis, I am ready;
Lead me to the Grove of Artemis.

Chorus Member

No!

Chorus Member

No!

Chorus Member

No!

Chorus Member

I cannot bear to listen.

Chorus Member

I cannot bear to look.

Chorus Member

You must –

Chorus Member

We must –

Chorus Member

One and all.

Klytaimnestra

Child, don't leave your mother like this.

Iphigeneia

I wish that I could stay awhile, but can't.

Klytaimnestra

Stay, stay, don't leave me.

Iphigeneia

I will not allow
One tear fall on my behalf.
So let us sing the hymn of sacrifice
To Zeus child, Artemis,
So my fate be fortunate for Greece.
Let us make ready holy reeds
And kindle cleansing fires,
Lead me to the altar;
I now bring salvation
And victory, victory, victory to Greece.

Iphigeneia

(*Sings.*)

Give me garlands for my head,
Plait my hair with flowers,
Death must be my marriage bed
But, by my death, revenge is ours.
Dance around the Danaan ships,
Dance in sacrificial bliss.
With my lifeblood wet your lips,
Bow to the will of Artemis.

Chorus

The tears we have we shed them now,
For Artemis does not allow
A sacrifice to spoil with tears
And sentimental human fears.

All

Dance around the Danaan ships,
Dance in sacrificial bliss.
With my lifeblood wet your lips,
Bow to the will of Artemis.

Iphigeneia

O Mycenae, my happy home,
To your halls I'll no more come.
Young girls who cry now for my fate
You must support me, celebrate.

All

Dance around the Danaan ships,
Dance in sacrificial bliss.
With my lifeblood wet your lips,
Bow to the will of Artemis.

Iphigeneia

O splendid sun, torchlight of our days,
Beacon of Zeus, I must now make my way
To darkness and eternal night
Fare you well, beloved light.

> (*To Black. KLYTAIMNESTRA alone. Enter
> AGAMEMNON.*)

Agamemnon

Woman? Wife?
Why do you weep?
Do you not hear?
Do you not see how all rejoice?
The winds begin to rise
We should be proud;
Our daughter is now one with Artemis,
The battlemaid of Greece.
She lives in the company of the gods.

You must go back to Mycenae now;
Look to your other children.
I must see to the setting sail.

Fare you well then, Klytaimnestra Anassa,
May the Gods walk with you, wife.

(*Turns and leaves KLYTAIMNESTRA alone on stage.*)

Klytaimnestra

What does my heart now whisper?
Dresses hanging lifegone in her empty room –
Agamemnon! Agamemnon Anax,
I'll be waiting.
You dare seat yourself at my table once again,
And I will dish you such desserts
As you have never dreamed.
You hear me; waiting, however long
To pay you back in full. And in kind.

(*Ten years later. Night. The roof of the palace at Mycenae,
the evening of AGAMEMNON's return from Troy.*)

Old Man

There. That's it.
The last storyscraps of an agewrinkled fool.
And since all other storytellers
Are longdeadburied now,
Let that be the last tragedy of all;
How we first dipped our hands
In our own children's blood.

But now the war at Troy is over.
Ten years. Ten long years
And we have won.
Peace is danced through all
The ruined ghetto streets
By the young girls of Chalkis –
Now just aging pullets starved of cocks,
Clucking in remembrance
Of dead men they never knew.
But we are free. We are at peace –
(*Chuckles to himself.*)

Agamemnon
(Off.)

Old man! Come quick!
She comes for me with a butcher's knife!

Old Man

At peace –

Agamemnon
(Off.)
Old Man! She cuts the air out of my life.

Old Man

At peace with all except ourselves.
When will we have blood enough?
(Yawns. Looks to the distance.)
Dawns white light cracks dark night.
And it is time to sleep.

Voice of Klytaimnestra
It whispers that! And that! And that!

Agamemnon
(Off. Dying.)

Old man.

Voice of Klytaimnestra
Listen Agamemnon, can't you hear them?
All the dead, they whisper revenge.

The End.